THIS BOYFRIEND CHRONICLE JOURNAL BELONGS TO

Jackie Alexandra Pemberton

It feels good to express how you feel and let go of certain emotions that you have been keeping inside of you for so long. So the first thing I want you to do is, write a letter to yourself, a promise of all the things that you are going to let go of. Anything that does not serve your purpose, that is not good for you mentally or does not help you grow. Let all of that shit go.

Dear Jackie _____,

Hey love I just wanted to take a moment and let you know what we will not accept anymore and what it is that we want. We want a man that is going to show up for you in all and any aspects; that is going to put you as a priority within his life as he knows all and respect you as the strong woman that you are. You want and deserve a man that is going to fully trust you and support you in your dreams, goals and aspirations that you have for yourself. You deserve greatness and should have a man thats going to show up for you, that will to not have to rush into being the man that he needs to be. Yet don't get this wrong you are not queen Sheeba & so you are fully aware that you will in return help your spouse in anyway that he needs help when his back is up against the wall. A weak and insecure man is not what you need, you need a man who knows himself and is truly ready to receive the love that you have to offer, while you both grow together and begin to start your tribe and family. So keep your head up his

5 goals for the year I am GOING to accomplish

~~start your own llc~~

- start one business
- Purchase your first home
- plan a family Reunion & execute

5 personal goals I am GOING to accomplish

- Read more
- take a trip alone
- continue to work on your mental health
- LOVE YOURSELF Completely
- Pay off one debt

BOYFRIEND CHRONICLES:

WE ARE NO LONGER FORCING CHEMISTRY WITH PEOPLE

Today I am grateful for…. my home, food on my table, a healthy body, the option to get help with my mental health. my career, support friends and family

What did I do to make myself happy today?

You didn't give up when things got tough at work. You allowed yourself to get through the day and not close off in a ball. you reached out for help.

What did I do to make someone else happy today?

I was there to help a friend through a tough situation. Listen and provide guidance the best way I knew how.

How can I love myself more today?

Take care of you first before you pour into others. make sure that you are at peace before giving your undivided attention as this cause anxiety for yourself.

If you had to create a hashtag describing your day it would be.

#another one
we all we got
NO PAIN NOGAIN

Cheers to focusing on me notes

MY OWN BOYFRIEND CHRONICLE
AFFIRMATION:

Today I am grateful for….

my home, friends + family, the Available
funds within my possession

What did I do to make myself happy today?

telling myself that this quarantine will not
get the best of me. I will work on me.

What did I do to make someone else happy today?

There for a friend and helped look for a
home.

How can I love myself more today?

Do things that make me happy today and
my future self proud.

If you had to create a hashtag describing your day it would be.

#COVID19 got you
#life is but a box of chocolate

Cheers to focusing on me notes

Don't let these troubling day get the best of you. You make the best of you for these next couple of days.

BOYFRIEND CHRONICLES:

PAY ATTENTION TO THE FRIENDS WHO SEE YOU GROWING AND ONLY BRING UP THE PERSON YOU USE TO BE

MY OWN BOYFRIEND CHRONICLE
AFFIRMATION:

Today I am grateful for….

for the supportive friends that I have seeing me through this COVID 19.

What did I do to make myself happy today?

Took # time to read to expand my knowledge.

What did I do to make someone else happy today?

Unsure as I haven't had human contact.

How can I love myself more today?

Take a moment to focus on me even if just for one moment.

If you had to create a hashtag describing your day it would be.

what the buck
sore throat sore body
something gotta give

Cheers to focusing on me notes

BOYFRIEND CHRONICLES:

PEOPLE WHO CARE ABOUT YOU WILL PUT THE EFFORT IN TO SHOW YOU JUST THAT

MY OWN BOYFRIEND CHRONICLE AFFIRMATION:

Today I am grateful for….

this may sound bad but I'm
grateful for me and showing up
for me and my happiness and overall health.

What did I do to make myself happy today?

I rearranged my room so that
when I wake up in the morning im
greeted by the sunrise

What did I do to make someone else happy today?

I was their for a friend in their
time of uncertainty in their love life.

How can I love myself more today?

Continue to keep making steps towards
your happiness one step at a time.

If you had to create a hashtag describing your day it would be.

\# yougogirl
\# every step you take

Cheers to focusing on me notes

Your starting to smile more and that looks good on you. Don't give that up. :)

MY OWN BOYFRIEND CHRONICLE
AFFIRMATION:

Today I am grateful for….

Ability to have help so I navigate through years of past trauma and conflict.

What did I do to make myself happy today?

I went outside and enjoyed seeing happiness behind people mask. I cleaned my bathroom, I took time out to buy my something that I've been craving.

What did I do to make someone else happy today?

I was there to listen during my friends troubles of life that have been hurting them.

How can I love myself more today?

Allow yourself to begin the work to work on your shadow work.

If you had to create a hashtag describing your day it would be.

#I see you
#okay I see you

Cheers to focusing on me notes

MY OWN BOYFRIEND CHRONICLE
AFFIRMATION:

Today I am grateful for….

What did I do to make myself happy today?

What did I do to make someone else happy today?

How can I love myself more today?

If you had to create a hashtag describing your day it would be.

Cheers to focusing on me notes

BOYFRIEND CHRONICLES:

LONELINESS AND UNHEALTHY ATTACHMENTS WILL HAVE YOU TOLERATING SOME SHIT YOU WOULD HAVE NEVER IMAGINED

MY OWN BOYFRIEND CHRONICLE AFFIRMATION:

Today I am grateful for….

What did I do to make myself happy today?

What did I do to make someone else happy today?

How can I love myself more today?

If you had to create a hashtag describing your day it would be.

Cheers to focusing on me notes

BOYFRIEND CHRONICLES:

YOU ARE NOT BOB THE BUILDER AND YOU CANNOT FIX EVERY BROKEN MAN THAT YOU FIND

MY OWN BOYFRIEND CHRONICLE AFFIRMATION:

Today I am grateful for….

What did I do to make myself happy today?

What did I do to make someone else happy today?

How can I love myself more today?

If you had to create a hashtag describing your day it would be.

Cheers to focusing on me notes

BOYFRIEND CHRONICLES:

YOU WILL ALWAYS BE WAY TOO MUCH FOR PEOPLE WHO ARE COMFORTABLE WITH THINKING SMALL

MY OWN BOYFRIEND CHRONICLE
AFFIRMATION:

Today I am grateful for….

What did I do to make myself happy today?

What did I do to make someone else happy today?

How can I love myself more today?

If you had to create a hashtag describing your day it would be.

Cheers to focusing on me notes

MY OWN BOYFRIEND CHRONICLE
AFFIRMATION:

Today I am grateful for….

What did I do to make myself happy today?

What did I do to make someone else happy today?

How can I love myself more today?

If you had to create a hashtag describing your day it would be.

Cheers to focusing on me notes

MY OWN BOYFRIEND CHRONICLE
AFFIRMATION:

Today I am grateful for….

What did I do to make myself happy today?

What did I do to make someone else happy today?

How can I love myself more today?

If you had to create a hashtag describing your day it would be.

Cheers to focusing on me notes

BOYFRIEND CHRONICLES:

THE LOSSES YOU TAKE ARE TO MAKE SPACE FOR THE WINS THAT GOD HAS FOR YOU

**MY OWN BOYFRIEND CHRONICLE
AFFIRMATION:**

Today I am grateful for….

What did I do to make myself happy today?

What did I do to make someone else happy today?

How can I love myself more today?

If you had to create a hashtag describing your day it would be.

Cheers to focusing on me notes

MY OWN BOYFRIEND CHRONICLE
AFFIRMATION:

Today I am grateful for….

What did I do to make myself happy today?

What did I do to make someone else happy today?

How can I love myself more today?

If you had to create a hashtag describing your day it would be.

Cheers to focusing on me notes

BOYFRIEND CHRONICLES:

BY LOVING MYSELF FIRST IT GRANTS ME THE ABILITY TO PROPERLY LOVE OTHERS

MY OWN BOYFRIEND CHRONICLE
AFFIRMATION:

Today I am grateful for….

What did I do to make myself happy today?

What did I do to make someone else happy today?

How can I love myself more today?

If you had to create a hashtag describing your day it would be.

Cheers to focusing on me notes

MY OWN BOYFRIEND CHRONICLE AFFIRMATION:

Today I am grateful for….

What did I do to make myself happy today?

What did I do to make someone else happy today?

How can I love myself more today?

If you had to create a hashtag describing your day it would be.

Cheers to focusing on me notes

BOYFRIEND CHRONICLES:

SELF HARM IS ALSO PUTTING
YOURSELF AROUND PEOPLE
AND PLACES THAT HURT YOU.
PROTECT YOUR PEACE.

MY OWN BOYFRIEND CHRONICLE
AFFIRMATION:

Today I am grateful for....

What did I do to make myself happy today?

What did I do to make someone else happy today?

How can I love myself more today?

If you had to create a hashtag describing your day it would be.

Cheers to focusing on me notes

BOYFRIEND CHRONICLES:

YOU ARE NOT ASKING FOR TOO MUCH YOU ARE JUST ASKING THE WRONG PEOPLE

MY OWN BOYFRIEND CHRONICLE AFFIRMATION:

Today I am grateful for....

What did I do to make myself happy today?

What did I do to make someone else happy today?

How can I love myself more today?

If you had to create a hashtag describing your day it would be.

Cheers to focusing on me notes

BOYFRIEND CHRONICLES:

EVEN IF IT'S WITH TEARS
ROLLING DOWN YOUR FACE, I
PRAY YOU ALWAYS HAVE THE
ABILITY TO WALK AWAY FROM
PEOPLE WHO MAKE YOU FEEL
LIKE YOU HAVE TO BEG FOR
LOVE

MY OWN BOYFRIEND CHRONICLE
AFFIRMATION:

Today I am grateful for….

What did I do to make myself happy today?

What did I do to make someone else happy today?

How can I love myself more today?

If you had to create a hashtag describing your day it would be.

Cheers to focusing on me notes

BOYFRIEND CHRONICLES:

THE MOMENT YOU BEGIN PUTTING YOURSELF FIRST, THERE WILL BE NO ROOM FOR PEOPLE TO TREAT YOU LIKE AN OPTION

**MY OWN BOYFRIEND CHRONICLE
AFFIRMATION:**

Today I am grateful for….

What did I do to make myself happy today?

What did I do to make someone else happy today?

How can I love myself more today?

If you had to create a hashtag describing your day it would be.

Cheers to focusing on me notes

BOYFRIEND CHRONICLES:

YEARS OF FALLING IN LOVE WITH EVERYONE ELSE, NOW IS THE TIME TO FALL IN LOVE WITH YOURSELF.

**MY OWN BOYFRIEND CHRONICLE
AFFIRMATION:**

Today I am grateful for....

What did I do to make myself happy today?

What did I do to make someone else happy today?

How can I love myself more today?

If you had to create a hashtag describing your day it would be.

Cheers to focusing on me notes

BOYFRIEND CHRONICLES:

SECURE YOUR SPIRITUAL BAG FIRST
ALL OTHER BAGS WILL COME INTO
YOUR LIFE NATURALLY
THAT IS WHAT HAPPENS WHEN YOU
CHASE PURPOSE OVER POPULARITY

MY OWN BOYFRIEND CHRONICLE
AFFIRMATION:

Today I am grateful for....

What did I do to make myself happy today?

What did I do to make someone else happy today?

How can I love myself more today?

If you had to create a hashtag describing your day it would be.

Cheers to focusing on me notes

BOYFRIEND CHRONICLES:

WE ARE NO LONGER ASSOCIATING LOVE WITH ANYTHING THAT CAUSES US TO LOWER OUR WORTH OR FORGET OUR VALUE

**MY OWN BOYFRIEND CHRONICLE
AFFIRMATION:**

Today I am grateful for....

What did I do to make myself happy today?

What did I do to make someone else happy today?

How can I love myself more today?

If you had to create a hashtag describing your day it would be.

Cheers to focusing on me notes

BOYFRIEND CHRONICLES:

IF IT WAS EASY EVERYONE WOULD BE DOING IT. YOU HAVE TO SHOW UP FOR YOUR DREAMS EVEN ON THE DAYS YOU ARE THE ONLY PERSON WHO CAN SEE THEM.

MY OWN BOYFRIEND CHRONICLE AFFIRMATION:

Today I am grateful for….

What did I do to make myself happy today?

What did I do to make someone else happy today?

How can I love myself more today?

If you had to create a hashtag describing your day it would be.

Cheers to focusing on me notes

BOYFRIEND CHRONICLES:

YOU CANNOT EXPECT PEOPLE TO TRULY UNDERSTAND SOMETHING THAT YOU ARE DOING FOR YOU

MY OWN BOYFRIEND CHRONICLE AFFIRMATION:

Today I am grateful for….

What did I do to make myself happy today?

What did I do to make someone else happy today?

How can I love myself more today?

If you had to create a hashtag describing your day it would be.

Cheers to focusing on me notes

BOYFRIEND CHRONICLES:

SOMETIMES THE THINGS WE WANT ARE NOT SCHEDULED TO ARRIVE UNTIL AFTER WE GET OUR SHIT TOGETHER

MY OWN BOYFRIEND CHRONICLE AFFIRMATION:

Today I am grateful for….

What did I do to make myself happy today?

What did I do to make someone else happy today?

How can I love myself more today?

If you had to create a hashtag describing your day it would be.

Cheers to focusing on me notes

BOYFRIEND CHRONICLES:

WHEN YOU'RE A GOOD PERSON
PEOPLE WILL ALWAYS RETURN BACK
TO YOU
SOMETIMES FOR YOUR VIBE OTHER
TIMES BECAUSE YOU HAVE MADE
YOURSELF SO ACCESSIBLE

MY OWN BOYFRIEND CHRONICLE
AFFIRMATION:

Today I am grateful for….

What did I do to make myself happy today?

What did I do to make someone else happy today?

How can I love myself more today?

If you had to create a hashtag describing your day it would be.

Cheers to focusing on me notes

BOYFRIEND CHRONICLES:

YOU CANNOT MANIFEST THE
BLESSINGS THAT YOU WANT SO
BADLY, IF YOU DO NOT APPRECIATE
THE PROCESS IT TAKES IN MEETING
GOD HALFWAY.

MY OWN BOYFRIEND CHRONICLE
AFFIRMATION:

Today I am grateful for….

What did I do to make myself happy today?

What did I do to make someone else happy today?

How can I love myself more today?

If you had to create a hashtag describing your day it would be.

Cheers to focusing on me notes

BOYFRIEND CHRONICLES:

START LOVING PEOPLE WITH THE LOVE THEY NEED AND NOT THE TYPE OF LOVE YOU WOULD WANT SOMEONE TO GIVE TO YOU

MY OWN BOYFRIEND CHRONICLE
AFFIRMATION:

Today I am grateful for….

What did I do to make myself happy today?

What did I do to make someone else happy today?

How can I love myself more today?

If you had to create a hashtag describing your day it would be.

Cheers to focusing on me notes

BOYFRIEND CHRONICLES:

INVEST IN ANY AND EVERYTHING THAT BRINGS YOU ONE STEP CLOSER TO LOVING YOURSELF A LITTLE MORE

**MY OWN BOYFRIEND CHRONICLE
AFFIRMATION:**

Today I am grateful for….

What did I do to make myself happy today?

What did I do to make someone else happy today?

How can I love myself more today?

If you had to create a hashtag describing your day it would be.

Cheers to focusing on me notes

BOYFRIEND CHRONICLES:

WHY SIT AROUND WAITING FOR SOMEONE TO BRING YOU FLOWERS WHEN YOU HAVE THE ABILITY TO GO OUT AND GET THEM YOURSELF

**MY OWN BOYFRIEND CHRONICLE
AFFIRMATION:**

Today I am grateful for….

What did I do to make myself happy today?

What did I do to make someone else happy today?

How can I love myself more today?

If you had to create a hashtag describing your day it would be.

Cheers to focusing on me notes

BOYFRIEND CHRONICLES:

ALLOW YOURSELF TO BE ALONE TO FIGURE OUT EXACTLY WHAT YOUR HEART HAS BEEN TRYING TO TELL YOU

MY OWN BOYFRIEND CHRONICLE
AFFIRMATION:

Today I am grateful for….

What did I do to make myself happy today?

What did I do to make someone else happy today?

How can I love myself more today?

If you had to create a hashtag describing your day it would be.

Cheers to focusing on me notes

BOYFRIEND CHRONICLES:

YOU DESERVE THE TYPE OF LOVE YOU DO NOT HAVE TO QUESTION AND THAT INCLUDES WITH FRIENDSHIPS

**MY OWN BOYFRIEND CHRONICLE
AFFIRMATION:**

Today I am grateful for….

What did I do to make myself happy today?

What did I do to make someone else happy today?

How can I love myself more today?

If you had to create a hashtag describing your day it would be.

Cheers to focusing on me notes

BOYFRIEND CHRONICLES:

HOW BEAUTIFUL IS IT THAT EVEN AFTER ALL THE THINGS YOU HAVE BEEN THROUGH, YOU STILL FIND THE STRENGTH TO KEEP GOING?

MY OWN BOYFRIEND CHRONICLE
AFFIRMATION:

Today I am grateful for….

What did I do to make myself happy today?

What did I do to make someone else happy today?

How can I love myself more today?

If you had to create a hashtag describing your day it would be.

Cheers to focusing on me notes

BOYFRIEND CHRONICLES:

HOW DO YOU EXPECT TO HEAL WHEN YOU KEEP GOING BACK TO THE PLACES THAT HAVE HURT YOU?

**MY OWN BOYFRIEND CHRONICLE
AFFIRMATION:**

Today I am grateful for….

What did I do to make myself happy today?

What did I do to make someone else happy today?

How can I love myself more today?

If you had to create a hashtag describing your day it would be.

Cheers to focusing on me notes

BOYFRIEND CHRONICLES:

THERE ARE SO MANY REASONS IN THIS WORLD TO BE HAPPY, STOP LETTING YOUR ONLY REASON BE BECAUSE OF ANOTHER PERSON.

MY OWN BOYFRIEND CHRONICLE
AFFIRMATION:

Today I am grateful for….

What did I do to make myself happy today?

What did I do to make someone else happy today?

How can I love myself more today?

If you had to create a hashtag describing your day it would be.

Cheers to focusing on me notes

BOYFRIEND CHRONICLES:

EVERYDAY LET GO OF SOME TOXIC SHIT AND ENJOY THE WEIGHT COMING OFF OF YOUR SHOULDERS TO BECOME THE PERSON YOU WERE MEANT TO BE

MY OWN BOYFRIEND CHRONICLE AFFIRMATION:

Today I am grateful for….

What did I do to make myself happy today?

What did I do to make someone else happy today?

How can I love myself more today?

If you had to create a hashtag describing your day it would be.

Cheers to focusing on me notes

BOYFRIEND CHRONICLES:

SURROUND YOURSELF AROUND PEOPLE WHO INSPIRE YOU TO STEP OUT OF YOUR COMFORT ZONE

MY OWN BOYFRIEND CHRONICLE
AFFIRMATION:

Today I am grateful for….

What did I do to make myself happy today?

What did I do to make someone else happy today?

How can I love myself more today?

If you had to create a hashtag describing your day it would be.

Cheers to focusing on me notes

BOYFRIEND CHRONICLES:

YOU DON'T SUCCEED BECAUSE OF LUCK
YOU SUCCEED BY BEING CONSISTENT WITH THE THINGS THAT YOU ARE PASSIONATE ABOUT AND REMEMBERING GOD IN THE MIST OF A LOST OR A VICTORY

MY OWN BOYFRIEND CHRONICLE
AFFIRMATION:

Today I am grateful for….

What did I do to make myself happy today?

What did I do to make someone else happy today?

How can I love myself more today?

If you had to create a hashtag describing your day it would be.

Cheers to focusing on me notes

BOYFRIEND CHRONICLES:

DISCOVER HOW VALUABLE TIME IS AND YOU WILL STOP LETTING PEOPLE WASTE YOURS

**MY OWN BOYFRIEND CHRONICLE
AFFIRMATION:**

Today I am grateful for….

What did I do to make myself happy today?

What did I do to make someone else happy today?

How can I love myself more today?

If you had to create a hashtag describing your day it would be.

Cheers to focusing on me notes

BOYFRIEND CHRONICLES:

NO MORE POURING FROM EMPTY CUPS OR ACCEPTING HALF ASS LOVE

MY OWN BOYFRIEND CHRONICLE
AFFIRMATION:

Today I am grateful for….

What did I do to make myself happy today?

What did I do to make someone else happy today?

How can I love myself more today?

If you had to create a hashtag describing your day it would be.

Cheers to focusing on me notes

MY OWN BOYFRIEND CHRONICLE
AFFIRMATION:

Today I am grateful for….

What did I do to make myself happy today?

What did I do to make someone else happy today?

How can I love myself more today?

If you had to create a hashtag describing your day it would be.

I am so proud of you, you have become the author of your own story, now you can decide how this love story with yourself will end.

09.29.2020 1533